P9-DEU-324

# WOMEN IN
# COMPUTER SCIENCE

by Tammy Gagne

MIDLOTHIAN PUBLIC
14701 S. KENTON AVENUE
MIDLOTHIAN, IL 60445

**Content Consultant**
Margrit Betke, PhD
Professor, Department of Computer Science
Boston University

**Core Library**

An Imprint of Abdo Publishing
abdopublishing.com

abdopublishing.com

Published by Abdo Publishing, a division of ABDO, PO Box 398166, Minneapolis, Minnesota 55439. Copyright © 2017 by Abdo Consulting Group, Inc. International copyrights reserved in all countries. No part of this book may be reproduced in any form without written permission from the publisher. Core Library™ is a trademark and logo of Abdo Publishing.

Printed in the United States of America, North Mankato, Minnesota
032016
092016

Cover Photo: Adrian Sherratt/Rex Features/AP Images
Interior Photos: iStockphoto, 4, 23, 29; Alvarez/iStockphoto, 7; Red Line Editorial, 8; Ann Ronan Pictures/Heritage Images/Glow Images, 10; Corbis, 13; AP Images, 16; Suzanne Plunkett/Bloomberg/Getty Images, 18; Steve Rogers Photography/Getty Images for SXSW/Getty Images, 21; Hello Lovely/Blend RM/Glow Images, 26; Shutterstock Images, 30; Chromatika Multimedia/Shutterstock Images, 31; Xaume Olleros/Bloomberg/Getty Images, 34; Heather Leiphart/News Herald/AP Images, 37, 43; Melanie Stetson Freeman/The Christian Science Monitor/Getty Images, 39, 45

Editor: Arnold Ringstad
Series Designer: Laura Polzin

**Cataloging-in-Publication Data**
Names: Gagne, Tammy, author.
Title: Women in computer science / by Tammy Gagne.
Description: Minneapolis, MN : Abdo Publishing, [2017] | Series: Women in
    STEM | Includes bibliographical references and index.
Identifiers: LCCN 2015960510 | ISBN 9781680782646 (lib. bdg.) |
    ISBN 9781680776751 (ebook)
Subjects: LCSH: Women in computer science--Juvenile literature. | Computer
    industry--Juvenile literature.
Classification: DDC 004--dc23
LC record available at http://lccn.loc.gov/2015960510

J
004
GAG

# CONTENTS

# CHAPTER ONE

# CODERS WANTED!

**M**any people have some type of computer today. Some have a desktop or laptop. Others have a tablet or smartphone filled with apps. People might even have more than one of these devices. Computer code and the people who write it make these amazing machines possible.

Code is a list of commands that a computer follows. Each command tells the computer to carry

Tablets put powerful computer technology into portable, easy-to-use devices.

out a specific task. A computer program is a long list of code. Web browsers, apps, and video games are examples of programs. Programs are often made up of thousands of lines of code. They are also known as software.

Code can be written in many different programming languages. Each language has its own special format and style. The people who use these languages are known as programmers or coders. Teams of coders work together to build programs. Coders give computers instructions they

Coders usually write programs on desktop or laptop computers.

can understand. These people also fix the code when errors occur.

Personal computers would not exist without code. The same is true of the Internet and video games. Coding has improved our daily lives. It helps bring us information and entertainment faster than ever. It has changed the way the world works.

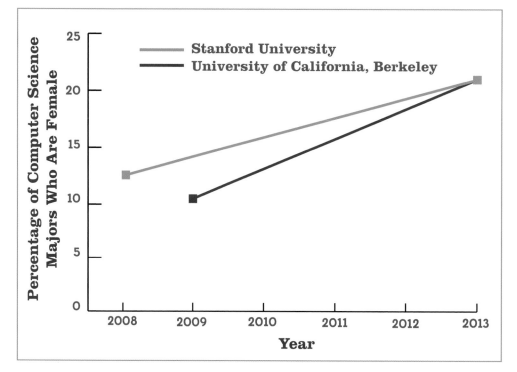

**Changes in Computer Science**

At Stanford University and the University of California, Berkeley, the number of women majoring in computer science has gone up. These graphs show the percentage of female computer science majors in the years shown. What do these numbers say about the future of women in computer science?

# Women and Coding

Women have made a major impact in the history of programming. But their numbers are relatively low. Women make up only a small percentage of coders. In 2013 about half the workers in the United States were women. But they held only 20.3 percent of coding jobs. The need for coders is growing fast. Companies are hiring many of them each year. Larger numbers of women are now entering the field.

Computer science is a rewarding career. Every day, coders use creativity and clever thinking to solve problems. Their programs may be used by millions of people around the world. Computer science also pays well. Many coders earn more than $80,000 per year. This is well above the national average among all jobs.

Women have accomplished great things in computer science. They know what interesting and exciting work it can be. Many of these women want to share their experiences with girls who are deciding what their future careers will be.

## In Demand

Coding jobs are on the rise. It looks as if more openings are coming. The Bureau of Labor Statistics predicts that the United States will have 1 million unfilled programming jobs by 2020. Many new programmers will be needed to fill these positions.

# CHAPTER TWO

# NO STRANGERS TO COMPUTER SCIENCE

More men than women work in computer science today. However, women are not new to this field. Women have been involved in computer science for longer than many people realize. In fact, many of the first computer programmers were women. Among them was Ada Lovelace.

Ada Lovelace was born in 1815. She was the daughter of English poet Lord Byron. Her mother

Ada Lovelace was one of the earliest computer science innovators.

insisted that she learn about math. Lady Byron saw math as more important than literature and poetry. As it turned out, Lovelace had the opportunity to mix creativity, math, and science.

At 17 years old, she began working with mathematician Charles Babbage. Babbage had an idea for a machine unlike any other of its time. He wanted to make a device that could solve complex math problems. Lovelace agreed that such a machine could be created. She knew it could do more than math. She imagined it producing words, pictures, and even music. Lovelace wrote notes on how one could instruct the machine to work. More than a century passed before these ideas became reality.

## Jean Jennings Bartik

Jean Jennings Bartik began her career in 1945 as a human computer. At the time, people performed the calculations that machines do now. These people were known as human computers. In the 1940s, they helped the US Army figure out trajectories

The earliest electronic computers filled entire rooms.

for cannons and rockets. This work was extremely important during World War II (1939–1945). The United States needed skilled human computers to help make their weapons as accurate as possible.

Soon Bartik was offered a new opportunity. An electronic computer was finally being built. The work was being done at the University of Pennsylvania. The machine was called ENIAC—short for Electronic Numerical Integrator and Computer. The men in charge of the project were building the computer hardware. The job of programming remained open. Bartik and five other women rose to

## IN THE REAL WORLD

### A Key Role

Jean Jennings Bartik did not have to compete against men for the job of programming ENIAC. At the time, programming was seen as less important than building the hardware. Luckily for the ENIAC project, many women had studied math in the 1930s. Bartik and her coworkers influenced the project more than expected. They told the hardware designers how they could improve the computer.

the challenge. They wrote the computer code for this innovative machine.

After the war, Bartik worked on improvements to ENIAC. She later made contributions to other early electronic computers. Bartik believed more gender diversity was needed in computer science. She encouraged women to participate in scientific careers.

## Margaret Hamilton

When most people think of the first moon landing, they think of Neil Armstrong and Buzz Aldrin. These men were the first two people to walk on the moon. But one of the most important

### COBOL

Coding pioneer Grace Hopper helped develop COBOL. This early programming language was invented in 1959. COBOL is short for Common Business-Oriented Language. It allowed coders to program computers using English words rather than a complex series of numbers. COBOL also made it possible for many companies to use the same software. This saved a lot of time and money.

Hamilton sits in a training version of the Apollo spacecraft.

keys to their success was the work of computer scientist Margaret Hamilton.

Hamilton worked at the Massachusetts Institute of Technology (MIT). She wrote the computer code for the moon-bound spacecraft. This code helped the Apollo 11 mission reach the moon.

The software she developed may have prevented a disaster. As the lunar lander spacecraft neared the surface, its computer began showing errors. It was overloaded with calculations. But Hamilton's software was designed to fix these errors by focusing on only the most important calculations. Thanks to Hamilton's software, the astronauts landed safely on the moon. Hamilton also came up with the term *software engineer*. This title is now used to describe men and women who design and write programs.

## EXPLORE ONLINE

The focus of Chapter Two is the history of women in computer science. The below article from Smithsonian.com is about the role women played in the history of coding. What new information can you learn from this website?

## Computer Programming Used to Be Women's Work

mycorelibrary.com/women-in-computer-science

# CHAPTER THREE

# TODAY'S TOP INNOVATORS

Computer coding has come a long way since its early days. Modern programmers have learned from the work of coders such as Bartik and Hamilton. Recent innovators are taking programming to amazing new levels. Technology that once seemed impossible is now in the hands of everyday people.

Caterina Fake cofounded the photo-sharing website Flickr with Stewart Butterfield.

# Caterina Fake

Caterina Fake was not drawn to programming as a youngster. But this did not stop her from succeeding in the field. As a child, Fake wanted to become an artist or a writer. In college she majored in English. After graduation, though, Fake changed her path. She decided to pursue a career in programming.

Fake taught herself how to program. She then got a job with a web design company. As part of that team, she helped create Flickr. The photo sharing service quickly became popular. Rather

## Women Are Good for Business

NCWIT stands for the National Center for Women & Information Technology. The NCWIT works to bring more women into technology fields. It is made up of more than 600 universities, companies, and other organizations. The group believes companies with more diversity solve problems better than those made up of one gender or ethnicity. According to the NCWIT, businesses with more gender diversity in management make more money than those without diversity.

More than 10 billion photos have been posted to Flickr since the website started in 2004.

## Making the Path Easier for Others

Daphne Koller is a computer science professor at Stanford University. She cofounded a project to bring education to anyone who wants to learn. It is called Coursera. The program lets people all over the world take online classes for free. Students complete homework assignments and are graded for their work. By 2015 Coursera involved more than 135 universities and more than 16 million students. Many students have used their new skills to get better jobs. Others have gotten college credit.

than writing stories, she became a professional at writing code.

## Jennifer Pahlka

Jennifer Pahlka is changing coding in a big way. She started out by working in the computer game industry for eight years. She later founded Code for America. The goal of this program is to improve government websites that are not making the most of technology. Working with one city at a time, Code for America has received help from approximately 16,000 coding volunteers.

Pahlka speaks to audiences about how coding can improve the world.

Pahlka's work with Code for America also led her to a job with the White House. As US deputy chief technology officer, she cofounded the US Digital Service. This team is helping the government keep up with advancing technology.

Pahlka also inspired something called civic hacking. When a problem arises in a community, local programmers use their skills to solve it. The coders meet with government workers, business owners, or local residents. Together they explore how coding might help make a difference.

Programmer Ellen Ullman shared her thoughts on success in computer science with the *New York Times*:

> *The first requirement for programming is a passion for the work, a deep need to probe the mysterious space between human thoughts and what a machine can understand; between human desires and how machines might satisfy them.*
>
> *The second requirement is a high tolerance for failure. Programming is the art of algorithm design and the craft of debugging errant code. In the words of the great John Backus, inventor of the Fortran programming language: "You need the willingness to fail all the time. You have to generate many ideas and then you have to work very hard only to discover that they don't work. And you keep doing that over and over until you find one that does work."*

Source: Ellen Ullman. "How to Be a Woman Programmer." New York Times. New York Times, May 18, 2013. Web. Accessed December 2, 2015.

## Back It Up

Take a close look at this text. What does Ullman think are the most important traits for a computer programmer? How is failure part of the path to success in coding?

# CHAPTER FOUR

# BUILDING A BETTER WORLD

Programming has solved many problems in the modern world. Some companies have offices in different regions. They can now use programs such as Skype or FaceTime to help employees communicate. Technology has also caused its fair share of problems. Computer viruses and identity theft are big issues. Fortunately, programmers also work to solve these problems. Women have made

Video chatting is one of many innovations made possible by coding.

## Going Mobile

Jeanine Swatton works at Yodlee Interactive. This company creates banking software. Swatton develops mobile iPhone and iPad apps for Yodlee. She also teaches coding for smartphone software in her spare time. Swatton loves writing code. Her passion for the work is what makes it so fun and easy for her. She also enjoys the feeling that comes from seeing one of her apps running on an iPhone.

an impact in this field of computer science as well.

# Radia Perlman

Radia Perlman invented a computer technology called spanning tree protocol (STP). STP played a major role in the development of the Internet. While the technology is complex, the effect is simple. Perlman made it easier for people to go where they want to go online.

Many people even call her the Mother of the Internet. Perlman doesn't like the nickname, though. She explains that the Internet is the result of many people's hard work.

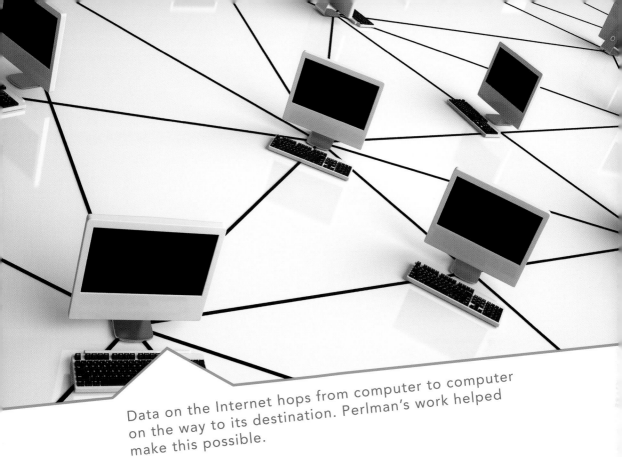

Data on the Internet hops from computer to computer on the way to its destination. Perlman's work helped make this possible.

One of the things that made Perlman so successful is her interest in solving problems. She enjoys looking at a problem from different angles. Perlman does not jump right in and write code to solve a small issue. Instead she takes time to think about the problem. Is the real issue a bigger problem? By asking herself this, she has devised simple coding solutions. Her fixes often end up solving many smaller problems as well as the big one.

```
<!DOCTYPE html>
<html>
<body>

<h1>Example Website Heading</h1>

<p>This is a sample paragraph on this website. It is made up of three sentences
and has some <b>bold text</b>. There is an image of a computer below it.</p>

<img src="computer.jpg" alt="Picture of a desktop computer">

</body>
</html>
```

# Example Website Heading

This is a sample paragraph on this website. It is made up of three sentences and has some **bold text**. There is an image of a computer below it.

## Code Is Communication

At first computer code looks like a jumble of letters, numbers, and other characters. Once a person learns what the commands mean, however, the code begins to make sense. Each command instructs the computer to perform a different action. Above is the behind-the-scenes code that makes up a web page. It is written in HTML. HTML tells a web browser what things to display. It is not a programming language, but it works together with programming languages to make exciting websites. Below the code is what would actually show up in a web browser. What part of the HTML code do you think tells the web browser to show an image?

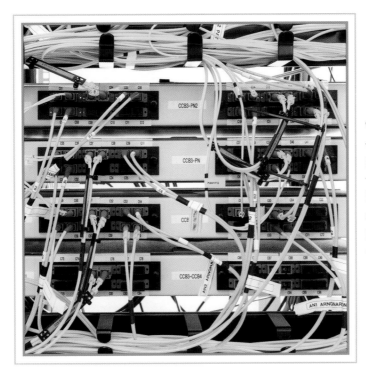

With so much data traveling freely between devices on the Internet, it is important to have strong security to protect against cyber attacks.

## Lixia Zhang

Lixia Zhang has helped make the Internet a safer place. This coding innovator did not begin her career as a programmer. Zhang's first job was driving a tractor on a farm in northern China. She came to the United States to study at MIT. She later became a professor at the University of California, Los Angeles, in the computer science department.

Zhang has created some of the most advanced technology in Internet security. She also invented the term *middlebox*. This word describes devices that inspect and filter Internet traffic. A firewall is an example of middlebox technology. It keeps a computer or network safe from users who intend to harm it.

## Barbara Liskov

Many people find coding more fun than many other science, technology, engineering, and math (STEM) jobs. MIT computer science professor Barbara Liskov is one of them. She took her first programming job because she couldn't find an interesting one in math. In addition to teaching, Liskov also works as a researcher. Her biggest goal is to improve software that people depend on every day. She won the 2008

### Getting Started

Kids interested in coding can learn the basics through apps created just for them. MIT staff and students developed a coding language called Scratch for students between the ages of 8 and 16. It even allows users to share their work online. The web-based program is free to use.

Turing Award for her work in programming languages. This is the top award in computer science.

Liskov's work includes research on fault tolerance. How can a computer keep working while tolerating a problem in one of its parts? Liskov realized that no one can completely prevent these problems from happening. Some errors will always occur. Liskov's goal is to prevent a few small problems from shutting down a whole system.

## FURTHER EVIDENCE

There is a lot of information about how coding can solve problems in Chapter Four. What was one of the chapter's main points? What evidence was given to support that point? Check out the link below. Choose a quote from the web page that relates to this chapter. Does this quote support the author's main point? Does it make a new point? Write a few sentences explaining how the quote you found relates to this chapter.

**Young Women Use Code to Solve Real-World Problems**
mycorelibrary.com/women-in-computer-science

# CHAPTER FIVE

# WOMEN AND THE FUTURE OF COMPUTER SCIENCE

Learning about the work of other coders is a great way to get started in computer science. Role models can inspire girls who hope to become computer programmers. The next step is to find resources that can help teach programming skills.

## Girls Who Code

In 2015 Georgetown University hosted its first Girls Who Code Summer Immersion Program in

More girls are learning to code today than ever before.

Washington, DC. Sixty girls from different high schools took part in the event. At the end of the course, the students presented their final projects. Each was an idea for a new app or website.

Similar programs have been created around the United States. A company called iD Tech runs coding camps for girls and boys at more than 150 locations. Younger kids can learn to create games with a programming tool called Tynker. Older students may prefer to work with the Python language.

Across the country, mentors are helping girls learn coding concepts.

## Working Together

Electrical engineer Kimberly Bryant founded Black Girls CODE. Her goal was to give young girls of color more opportunities to learn about programming. The organization sponsors events in which girls work together to solve problems by writing code. Girls entering grades 6 through 12 are encouraged to participate in these gatherings. All experience levels are welcomed. Mentors guide the teams through the three-day event.

## Everyday Learning

Girls who attend Prairie Crossing Charter School in Grayslake, Illinois, do not have to wait until summer to learn coding. In 2015 the school started its own Girls Who Code chapter. The afterschool program teaches programming skills to girls.

Other Girls Who Code programs exist all over the United States, from Massachusetts to California. Some of the biggest tech companies support the organization. AT&T, Adobe, and other businesses have donated $2.7 million to the project. At the end of 2015, Girls Who Code had educated approximately 10,000 girls

The computer science students of today will build the amazing apps and programs of the future.

in 40 different states. This is the same number of women who graduated from college with computer science degrees in that year.

## A Girls—and Boys—Club

Women in computer programming work alongside men in their jobs. Many girls learn coding alongside boys as well. Google has joined forces with the Boys & Girls Clubs of America to expand its afterschool coding programs. The programs welcome kids between the ages of 9 and 14. More than 120,000 boys and girls have participated in the programs. With the help of the Boys & Girls Clubs of America, Google hopes to increase this number.

The next time you use a computer, think about all the women who helped make modern computers possible. Keep in mind that many innovative coders are working today. You or your friends might create the computer science breakthroughs of tomorrow.

Linda Liukas writes and illustrates a children's book series that teaches kids about coding. A programming language called Ruby is depicted as a six-year-old girl in the books. Liukas was interviewed for a newspaper article in 2015:

> If the idea of a book about digital ideas seems strange—surely an app would be more apt?—it is important to note Liukas doesn't think children should spend all their time in front of a screen. She just wants them to spend more time thinking about how to use computers as tools to change the world. "I ask kids to build computers out of paper, or design an app by hand," she says. "It's about imagination."
>
> Liukas is working on Ruby's future adventures: in the last few years a new coding language, called Julia, has been developed in America and is gaining prominence. Liukas aims to incorporate it into her books. "Julia will be Ruby's friend," she says.

*Source: Rebecca Burn-Callander. "Why Women Make Gifted Coders." The Telegraph. The Telegraph, June 6, 2015. Web. Accessed December 17, 2015.*

## What's the Big Idea?

Take a close look at this text. What is the main point? Pick out two details used to make this point. What can you tell about coding based on this text?

GETTING INVOLVED

## Become a Girl Who Codes

Does your city have a Girls Who Code chapter? If not, talk to your mathematics or computer science teacher about the possibility of starting one. Visit the organization's website to see what it takes.

## Brainstorm

Think of apps that you wish existed. Next, go over the list and select the idea you think is the best. How would you go about creating it yourself? What would be the first step?

## Start from Scratch

Visit the website MIT created for its Scratch programming platform. Read about what Scratch can do and then give it a try. Share what you create with others in the Scratch community.

## Learning Languages

Find a book or website about different kinds of
programming languages. Learn what common languages
are used for. Which languages seem the most interesting to
you? Which ones might you like to learn?

## Surprise Me

Chapter One shared some interesting information about how coding affects our everyday lives. List two or three facts from the chapter that you found surprising. Why did they surprise you?

## Why Do I Care?

Many people use technology every day. But only a small percentage of those people know how to create it or fix it when a problem arises. What are some of the advantages of knowing how to code? How could you use this kind of knowledge to help people?

## Tell the Tale

Imagine you have traveled back in time to meet Ada Lovelace. How would you explain modern computers to her? How would you explain such concepts as code, apps, and tablets?

## You Are There

Imagine you are a computer programmer. What kinds of programs would you like to write? Smartphone apps? Video games? Make a list of all the things you might create using coding.

# GLOSSARY

**algorithm**
a step-by-step method for solving a problem

**app**
a computer program that runs on a smartphone or tablet

**code**
a list of instructions that a computer follows

**diversity**
having people from a variety of different backgrounds

**firewall**
a system that keeps a computer network safe from users who intend to steal information or disrupt the network

**influential**
having a significant effect

**innovator**
a person who does something new or in a new way

**trajectory**
the curve that an object travels along in air or space

# LEARN MORE

## Books

Briggs, Jason R. *Python for Kids*. San Francisco, CA: No Starch Press, 2014.

Marji, Marjed. *Learn to Program with Scratch*. San Francisco, CA: No Starch Press, 2014.

McManus, Sean. *How to Code in 10 Easy Lessons*. London: Walter Foster, Jr., 2015.

## Websites

To learn more about Women in STEM, visit **booklinks.abdopublishing.com**. These links are routinely monitored and updated to provide the most current information available.

Visit **mycorelibrary.com** for free additional tools for teachers and students.

# INDEX

# ABOUT THE AUTHOR

Tammy Gagne has written more than 100 books for both adults and children. She resides in northern New England with her husband and son. One of her favorite pastimes is visiting schools to talk to children about the writing process.